HASSLE-FREE HOME SECURITY

HASSLE-FREE
HOME SECURITY

BILL PHILLIPS

DOUBLEDAY BOOK & MUSIC CLUBS, INC.
GARDEN CITY, N.Y.

Printed in the United States of America
ISBN 1-56865-058-2
Illustrations by Marta Cone
Book design by Peter R. Kruzan
Art direction by Diana Klemin
GuildAmerica Books® is a registered trademark of Doubleday Book & Music Clubs, Inc.

To Gloria Glenn

ACKNOWLEDGMENTS

Special thanks to Jane Jordan Browne, Merlyn Coles, Oscar Ondra Carr, Daniel Phillips and Michael Phillips for their hard work and inspiration that made this book possible.

Thanks also to the many agencies and organizations that provided me with invaluable information, among them: the Canadian Centre for Justice Statistics, Federal Emergency Management Agency, the International Association of Home Safety and Security Professionals, U.S. Fire Administration, National Fire Sprinkler Association, U.S. Department of Justice and Underwriters Laboratories.

TABLE OF CONTENTS

WHAT YOU DON'T KNOW CAN HURT YOU.   1

1. BURGLARY 101: WHAT BURGLARS KNOW.   5
The secret to keeping burglars out.

2. LOCKS BURGLARS HATE. How locks are defeated.   10
The truth about lockpicking. Making a weak lock strong.
Professional Tips. Lock Buyer's Checklist. Resource list.

3. DOORS FOR STRENGTH AND BEAUTY. How to   21
make any door stronger. Door hardware. Garage doors.
Door Buyer's Checklist. Resource list.

4. WINDOWS THAT KEEP BURGLARS OUT.   28
Dealing with glass problems. Using security film. Buying
window hardware. Resource list.

5. BURGLAR ALARMS: DO YOU REALLY NEED   36
ONE? Special features to look for. Professional
installation vs. do-it-yourself models. Hidden fees you
should know about. Monitoring an alarm. Burglar Alarm
Buyer's Checklists. Resource list.

6. THE SAFEST SAFES. Why some aren't safe.   47
Deciding if you need one. Getting the best buy. Safe
alternatives. Safe Buyer's Checklist. Resource list.

CONTENTS

7. LIGHTING YOUR WAY TO SAFETY. Outdoor and indoor lighting. Motion activated lights. Home Lighting Checklist. Resource list. — 55

8. HIGH-TECH/LOW-COST SECURITY. Affordable closed circuit TVs. Answering your door when you're away. Catching crooks by phone. Resource list. — 61

9. LEARN NOT TO BURN. Designing an escape plan. Fire fighting techniques. Choosing smoke detectors, fire extinguishers and sprinkler systems. Fire Hazards Checklist. Resource list. — 68

10. DOING BUSINESS AT HOME SAFELY. Home Office Security. Resource list. — 78

11. GETTING INSURANCE JUST IN CASE . . . How to buy maximum coverage at minimum cost. Finding the right agent. Federal Crime Insurance. Resource list. — 82

12. APARTMENT HUNTER'S SECURITY CHECKLIST. — 90

13. BEFORE GOING ON VACATION. — 93

14. TOP 20 NO-COST SECURITY MEASURES. — 96

15. CONDUCTING YOUR OWN HOME SECURITY SURVEY. Professional Tips. Security Survey Checklist. — 101

16. RESOURCE DIRECTORY. Sources of Security Products. Using the Yellow Pages. U.S. Cities Ranked by Burglary Risk. Canadian Provinces/Territories Ranked by Burglary Risk. — 106

WHAT YOU DON'T KNOW CAN HURT YOU

Some people think common sense is all you need to stay safe at home. When they hear that someone was attacked by an intruder, they wonder why the victim didn't grab a baseball bat. When they hear that someone died in a fire, they wonder why the person didn't just run out of the house.

Among industrialized countries the United States has the highest yearly rate of fire deaths (Canada has the second highest). Over seventy-five percent of the deaths occur in homes. Each year members of one in four U.S. and Canadian households experience a rape, assault or theft.

If staying safe at home were just a matter of using common sense, there wouldn't be so many victims. Everyone would like to fight back against crime, but many people find out too late that they really don't know how.

Common sense doesn't tell you when (or how) to stay in your bedroom during a fire. Nor does it tell you why some locks that sell for under twenty dollars are better than others costing over one hundred dollars.

While working throughout the United States as a locksmith, safe technician and alarm-systems installer, I've seen intelligent people waste a lot of money doing incredibly stupid things trying to stay safe. Because I've tested and written about hundreds of security products for *Consumers Digest, Home Mechanix* and other magazines, I know which products work and which don't.

In this compact, easy-to-read book I tell you everything you need to know to stay safe and protect your property at home— without spending a lot of time or money. Subjects I cover include protecting a home office, getting more home insurance for less money, keeping your home secure while you vacation, choosing and using fire safety equipment, finding a safe apartment. . . .

Do you remember the parents who secretly used videotape to catch a babysitter beating their infant? I'll show you several ways you too can use surveillance equipment and other high-tech security devices at little cost.

I also tell you how to get the best buys on locks, safes, alarms, windows, doors, lights and other security products—and how to make the most out of what you have.

I include handy checklists and charts throughout the book. I also include addresses and toll-free phone numbers for getting free catalogs, booklets and literature.

Whether you live in a large city, suburb or rural area you'll find lots of information you can immediately use. I've used many of these tips and suggestions while living in cities as diverse as New York, Albuquerque, New Mexico and Springfield, Ohio.

My tips and suggestions are just as effective in Canada as in the United States, because these countries share proportionately similar crime and fire problems. (The Resource Directory includes names and addresses of manufacturers and suppliers in both countries.)

One last thing. This book is designed so you'll learn a lot even if you read only the chapters you're most interested in, but you'll get more out of it if you read the book straight through.

1.

BURGLARY 101:
WHAT BURGLARS KNOW

Much of this book focuses on thwarting burglars, because they're better than other criminals at breaking into a home. If you keep burglars out, you also keep rapists, vandals and other intruders out.

You may have heard people say: "If someone really wants to break into your home there's no way to stop him." But think about it for a minute. Could you break into any home and get out unnoticed if you wanted to? I know I couldn't. And most crooks couldn't either.

Many people give burglars more credit than they deserve. Some homeowners, for example, don't bother to lock doors because they think any burglar can just pick open the lock. (See more about lockpicking in Chapter 2.) But contrary to television crime dramas, few burglars are experienced locksmiths or former secret agents able to get into any place at any time. Most burglars are just opportunists who take advantage of a person's naïveté.

TYPES OF BURGLARS

There are three types of burglars: professional, semiprofessional and amateur. The top-notch professional is the one television crime dramas nearly always portray.

The old series "It Takes a Thief," for example, showed Alexander Mundy (played by Robert Wagner) thoughtfully planning and executing break-ins. He often used electronic devices, power tools and wall-climbing tools.

As in television shows and movies, the professional burglar is very skillful and may spend days or weeks planning a burglary. Given enough time, a professional can break into virtually any home. But he rarely does. Because he wants to get the most for his time and effort, the professional prefers breaking into businesses. He will break into a home only if he thinks valuables are in it.

The semiprofessional is less picky. He knows only a few tricks to get into buildings, and will break into any place where those tricks can be successfully used. He usually breaks into homes, because businesses are more secure. Semiprofessionals who are gang members or drug addicts can be dangerous.

The amateur doesn't actively look for opportunities to steal, but takes advantage of a situation that pops up. The amateur burglar is your next door neighbor who notices that your door is unlocked when no one is home. She quickly walks in and grabs some money or small items.

A statement like, "if someone really wants to break into your home there's no way to stop him" is true only for top-notch professional burglars. Unless you have a Van Gogh hanging in your living room—and have told a lot of people about it—you probably don't need to worry about professionals.

The biggest threat to most people who work for a living are semiprofessional and amateur thieves. Throughout this book, you'll learn simple ways to stop both types.

SEPARATING FACT FROM FICTION

Some people protect their homes against burglary during the day, but not at night. Others think break-ins occur only to businesses and rich people. Such naïveté can increase a person's risk of being burglarized.

Two out of every three burglaries that occur in the United States are residential. Half occur during the day, and half at night. (I'm not mentioning Canadian statistics because they're virtual mirror images of those for the United States.)

Throughout the nation burglary victims suffer $3.5 billion each year in losses, but the average loss per residential burglary is only $1,143. Households earning less than ten thousand dollars per year have higher burglary rates than households earning more.

As you probably suspected, homes in central cities have higher burglary rates than those in suburban and nonmetropolitan areas, but you may be surprised to learn that such major cities as Los Angeles, New York and Chicago have lower burglary rates than many smaller cities (see Resource Directory).

These statistics show that anyone, anywhere, is a potential burglary victim. And if you're burglarized, you probably won't get your property back. Of the burglaries reported to law enforcement officials each year, only about fourteen percent are cleared. That's why it's important to take intelligent steps to keep burglars out.

THE SECRET TO KEEPING BURGLARS OUT

You can't stop people from burglarizing homes. But you can keep them from burglarizing yours.

Most burglars try to make rational decisions about which places to break into. They consider what valuables are in the building, and how easily they can get in and out without getting caught. A typical home burglary is completed in less than ten minutes.

The secret to deterring burglars is to convince them that the risk of getting caught outweighs the possible rewards. There are two basic ways to do that: give them no reason to think you have more valuables than do other people near you, and make your home hard to break into surreptitiously.

Throughout this book you'll learn many ways to keep burglars out. More importantly, you'll learn how to think like a home security expert. That will allow you to come up with creative security measures that are perfect for your situation. You'll then be able to thwart virtually any burglar—even one who has read this book.

2.

LOCKS BURGLARS HATE

As I pointed out in Chapter 1, most home burglars are opportunists. They look for places they can get into and out of within ten minutes without being seen. They usually have plenty of choices, because the locks on many homes can be defeated within three minutes.

Simply by using effective locks, you'll cause many burglars to pass by your home. When you know how burglars defeat locks, you'll know why they like some better than others and you'll be able to strengthen any lock you have.

THE KEY-IN-KNOB

The most popular door lock is the key-in-knob, which is shaped like two connecting doorknobs. New home builders prefer the lock because it's inexpensive and easy to install. Homeowners like it because they can quickly lock doors without keys (just by pulling them closed). Burglars like it because it lets them quickly unlock a door—without a key.

A key-in-knob is especially vulnerable, because after knocking one of the knobs off (with a hammer or brick), a burglar can open the lock with a screwdriver. This applies whether the key-in-knobs cost ten dollars or hundreds of dollars.

There are also many quiet ways to defeat such locks. That's why few things catch a home burglar's attention faster than a door with a lone key-in-knob. If a door leading into your home is secured only by a key-in-knob, add a stronger lock above it. That will give you a good combination of protection and convenience.

DEADBOLTS

Like most security professionals, I think a deadbolt lock is the most cost-effective supplement for key-in-knobs. The deadbolt is less vulnerable to several forms of attack, but not all deadbolts are created equal.

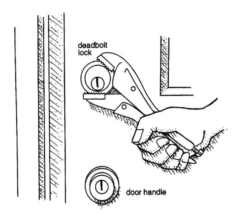

deadbolt
lock

door handle

Fig. 1

The strength of a deadbolt (or any lock) depends on how well it can resist all common forms of attack. Deadbolts are commonly attacked by jimmying, sawing, wrenching (see fig. 1) and kicking.

Jimmying is using a pry bar (or large screwdriver) to pry a door far enough away from its frame to free a lock's bolt. The longer the bolt, the harder the lock will be to jimmy. When you buy a deadbolt, make sure its bolt is at least one-inch long.

Most bolts are made of brass—an easy metal to cut. Therefore, deadbolts can also be attacked by inserting a hacksaw blade between the door and frame and sawing the bolt off. You should look for bolts made of hardened steel, or that have hardened steel inserts.

Some deadbolts can be defeated by using a wrench to forcibly twist the cylinder (the part with a keyway) to its open position. You can prevent that by buying a deadbolt with a tapered free-spinning cylinder guard. That device (it's included on most deadbolts) hinders a wrench from gripping the cylinder.

But few burglars walk around with pry bars, saw blades and wrenches. The method of forced entry most burglars use is the flying jump kick. It's fast, reliable and requires no special tools. One well-placed kick can break a lock's bolt (if it's brass), or rip the strike plate out of the doorframe.

STRIKE PLATES US. STRIKE BOXES

A standard strike plate is a thin piece of metal that's attached to a doorframe by two small screws. The best way to prevent kick-ins is to use a high-security strike box made of heavy-gauge steel with steel rods or three-inch screws (see fig. 2). It fits into a cutout on the doorframe (in the same place a strike plate would be installed),

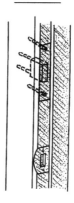

Fig. 2

and its rods or screws extend into a two-by-four stud in the wall. This helps hold a lock's bolt securely in place.

Using a high-security strike box is the best way to strengthen your deadbolt. Some deadbolts come with one, but most don't. You can buy a high-security strike box from a locksmith shop for between five and twenty dollars.

HIGHEST SECURITY LOCKS FOR HOMES

Most modern door locks are small and stylish. They can offer plenty of protection for a typical home, but not for homes in major cities or high-crime neighborhoods.

In places where some people routinely act uncivilized, aesthetics can play no part in choosing a lock. The lock must be so strong that, in effect, it welds a door and frame to the house.

The brace lock is one of the strongest (and ugliest) locks you can buy for a home. (In the movie *Burglar,* Whoopi Goldberg's character had a brace lock in her apartment—and the police officer who tried to kick in her door limped away in agony.) The lock is made for doors that open inward; it works on the same principle as a chair back braced under a doorknob.

The brace lock consists of a small rectangular box mounted on a door's interior side, a strike plate bolted to the floor, and a steel bar. One end of the steel bar is attached to the strike plate and the other clamps into the box. This braces the door closed. The door can be unlocked from the outside with a key.

WHAT ABOUT LOCKPICKING?

Lockpicking is the use of special tools to copy the action of a key. Although anyone can use a pick-key to open certain types of padlocks, most door locks are harder to pick open. Lockpicking tools for door locks don't work automatically; using them is a sophisticated skill that takes a long time to master.

You may have seen television crime dramas where the star uses a pick like a key to quickly open doors. That can't be done in real life. Picking a door lock open requires two tools, two steady hands and lots of concentration.

With a key, all of a lock's tumblers are automatically aligned to the open position. With picks, each tumbler has to be individually moved into place. An experienced locksmith can take from three to ten minutes picking open a door lock.

The main purpose of lockpicking is to open a door without damaging it or the lock. Burglars seldom resort to lockpicking because they don't mind damaging property. They only want to get in as fast as possible.

But if you live in a large city or near a high-crime area, you may need to worry about lockpicking. Such places often have more than their share of sophisticated burglars.

You can make any lock virtually unpickable by replacing its standard cylinder with a UL-listed one (many expensive locks come with a UL-listed cylinder). The UL listing means sample models have withstood rigorous expert attack tests against picking and other sophisticated methods of attack in accordance with Underwriters Laboratories guidelines.

LOCK AND FIRE SAFETY

Locks come in two styles: single and double cylinder. The double-cylinder models operate from both sides of a door with a key. Single cylinders use a key only on the outside, and a thumb-turn (or button) on the inside.

Some security professionals suggest using a double-cylinder lock on doors that have glass. They say if a thief breaks the glass, he won't be able to reach in and unlock the door. Or, if he gets in through a window, he'll have to leave through the window.

But only the dumbest of burglars wouldn't be able to get out through a door with a double-cylinder lock. If he couldn't find a screwdriver in the house, he could use a kitchen knife to remove the lock.

I don't recommend using double cylinders, because locking yourself in your house is dangerous. In an emergency—such as a fire—you have to search for a key to get out. What if you always keep the key in an easy-to-reach place? I've known people who've burned to death while holding a key.

There are better ways to deal with the problem of glass in a door. Plenty of alternatives to double-cylinder locks are included in Chapters 3 and 4.

PROFESSIONAL TIPS

1. The numbers and letters on the keys that come with a lock are codes that allow you to get new keys made over the phone. But a thief who sees the code can also get a key made. Whenever you buy a new lock, make duplicate keys and only carry the duplicates with you. (A duplicate key may also have numbers and letters, but they aren't codes for making a key.)

2. When you receive copies of a key, ask the locksmith to stamp "Do Not Duplicate" on them. (In some cities it's illegal for a

locksmith to copy such a stamped key without getting identification and keeping a log of the customer's name and address.)

3. Whenever you lose a key, immediately have the lock rekeyed so the old keys won't operate it anymore.

4. When you have a lock with a standard cylinder rekeyed, ask the locksmith to use two mushroom, or spool, pins. They will make the lock more pick resistant, and you probably won't be charged extra for them.

5. For convenience, have all the locks on an entry door operate on the same key. There's no security advantage in using more than one key for a door. In fact, having to fumble around for different keys can be dangerous at night.

6. Although some lock manufacturers claim otherwise, no UL-listed cylinder offers a home greater security than another UL-listed one. The lowest priced model is just as useful as the most expensive model.

LOCK BUYER'S CHECKLIST

For the lowest prices, buy standard locks at a hardware or department store. If you need one with a UL-listed cylinder, you may have to go to a locksmith. Use this checklist to get the most value for your money.

Deadbolt

Does the bolt have a one-inch throw?

Is the bolt hardened steel, or does it have a hardened steel insert?

Does the lock use a tapered free-spinning cylinder guard?

Does the lock come with a high-security strike box? (If not, add the cost of buying one.)

Are three-inch screws included for the strike plate or box?

Is the lock UL listed? (Important if you need high resistance to lockpicking.)

RESOURCES

The companies listed below are among the largest and most popular manufacturers of high-security locks and door hardware. Most sell their products through locksmiths and hardware stores, and not directly to consumers. You may want to contact them for literature and for the names of suppliers in your area. (Addresses and phone numbers are shown in The Resource Directory.)

High-Security Locks

Abloy Security Inc.

Assa High Security Locks

Medeco Security Locks, Inc.

Mul-T-Lock Corp. (USA)

New England Door and Lock Co., The

Schlage Lock Co.

High-Security Strike Boxes

Don-Jo Mfg.

M.A.G. Eng. & Mfg. Co., Inc.

Meister Atlanta Corp.

3.

DOORS FOR STRENGTH AND BEAUTY

A strong lock and strike box will hold up during a kick-in attack. But what good are they if a burglar's foot goes through the door? All the hardware in the world can't substitute for a strong door.

If strength were your only concern, you could just replace all your exterior doors with iron safe doors (and use brace locks). But that would be costly, unsightly and unnecessary.

Nearly any door can provide good security if it's properly reinforced. In this chapter I explain why some doors are stronger than others, and how you can make any door stronger. I also tell you the most common ways burglars bypass locks to get through doors.

DOOR CONSTRUCTION

How strong a door is depends on its material and construction. Common materials include wood, metal and glass. Common constructions include solid-core, hollow and panel.

The strongest doors are at least $1^3/_4$-inches thick and made of heavy steel (at least $1/_{64}$ inch) with a steel frame. Calamine doors (those made of metal wrapped over solid-core wood) offer good protection. Solid-core hardwood doors are also good if they're at least $1^3/_4$-inches thick.

A wood panel offers only poor to medium protection, because it has sections (or "panels") that are thinner than other parts of the door. The thin sections are nice to look at, but are also easier to kick-in than the thicker parts of the door.

In general, steel panel doors are better than wood panel doors. The worst door, however, is a hollow-core wood type. It's like one large super-thin panel.

Some security professionals recommend reinforcing a hollow-core door with a sheet of steel or heavy plywood. This might help, but it's a lot of work and the door will look strange. It's simply better not to use a hollow-core door as an exterior door.

GLASS IN DOORS

Glass in doors presents special problems—it can be broken and it allows thieves to see into your home. Many of the solutions are the same as those for window problems, which are detailed in Chapter 4. In addition, sliding glass doors can be troublesome because they're designed with a tiny lock that can be easily forced open and their aluminum frames can be bent or lifted off their tracks.

You can do three things to secure a sliding glass door: add a stronger lock, wedge a broomstick or thick rod in its track and install an antilift bar.

DOOR REINFORCEMENTS

Most wood doors are weakened over the years through chipping, splitting and new lock holes. You can strengthen a wood door by using a U-shaped steel reinforcement (see fig. 3) that fits over the edge of a door near the lock. For aesthetic purposes, door reinforcements come in the same colors as locks.

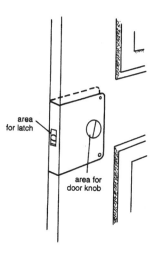

area
for latch

area for
door knob

Fig. 3

HINGES

If your exterior (or "entry") doors swing into the house, their hinges are probably inside your home. That's good. But if the doors swing outside the house, the hinges are probably on the outside and can be tampered with or removed by an intruder.

There are two things you can do about the problem: use high security hinges that have nonremovable pins or have a locksmith or carpenter adjust the door to open inward.

DOORFRAMES

If the hinges are on the inside of your house, you don't need to worry about them. But you may need to be concerned with something else.

If you face the side of your door where you can't see the hinges, you'll notice a protruding strip along the length of the lock side. That strip is the doorstop. It keeps the door from swinging past the frame when you close it.

If the doorstop is a solid part of the frame, that's good. But if it's attached with nails, you have a security problem (see fig. 4). A burglar can pry it off the doorframe to expose the lock bolts. That will make it easier to jimmy or saw the bolts.

You can make a removable doorstop stronger by prying it off and putting it back on with wood glue and nails. Then you might want to paint it and the frame so no one will know the doorstop wasn't built into the frame.

GARAGES

When planning for security, a garage that's attached to a house should be treated as part of the house. In most cases, the main door of a garage can be easily forced open.

Once a burglar gets into the garage, your neighbors won't be able to see him while he works on the door that leads into your

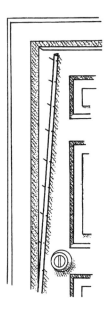

Fig. 4

house. If he drives into the garage, the burglar will also be able to leisurely pile your property into his car.

Like other exterior doors, a garage door should be strong. Thin or broken panels should be reinforced or replaced. The best way to secure a garage is to use an electronic garage door opener.

And make sure that the door connecting your house to your garage is as strong as the front door to your house.

RESOURCES

Doors

Peachtree Doors, Inc.

Pease Industries, Inc.

Pella Doors and Windows

Pinecrest

Simpson Door Co.

Hinges

Brookfield Industries, Inc.

Roton Corp.

Stanley Hardware

Reinforcements

Don-Jo Mfg., Inc.

M.A.G. Eng. & Mfg. Co., Inc.

Meister Atlanta Corporation

4.

WINDOWS THAT KEEP BURGLARS OUT

Next to doors, windows are the most popular entry point for burglars. Windows are vulnerable not only because they can be broken, but also because they let a burglar look inside a home. In addition, some types of windows can be easily opened from outside.

The windows you have were probably chosen to match the architectural style of your home. Replacing them with different types may look odd. Fortunately, like doors, all window types can be upgraded to provide adequate security in most cases.

TYPES OF WINDOWS

Double-hung, sliding glass, louvered and casement are the most common window types for homes.

A double hung consists of two sashes (or "frames"), one above the other; it is opened and closed by sliding the sashes up and down. A big problem with most models is they can be opened from outside a home by inserting a thin knife between the sashes and working the thumb-twist lock open.

To make a double hung more secure, supplement the thumb-twist with a lock that can't be opened from outside the home. The best locks are also the least expensive; they look like two screws and are inserted into two holes you drill in the sashes. Locks that require keys are expensive, unnecessary and potentially dangerous. They make a double hung hard to use during a fire or other emergency.

A sliding glass window is basically a double-hung window that's turned on it's side. It slides left and right rather than up and down.

Like a sliding glass door, it's vulnerable to being lifted off its track and should be secured by placing a broomstick into the bottom track.

A jalousie (or "louvered") window is the least secure type of window. It consists of a vertical row of slightly overlapping rectangular glass panes. The panes can easily be removed from the outside. Gluing the panels to the brackets will help a little. A better way to protect a jalousie window is to use metal grates or bars.

A casement window swings out like a door and is opened and closed with a crank. You may have seen a set of them on the sides of a picture or bay window. The big problem with a casement window is that if it's opened even a little, a burglar may be able to reach in and crank the window open wide enough to climb in. Better models use easily removable cranks.

To protect a casement window, never open the window more than a few inches and always remove the crank.

GLASS PROBLEMS

The biggest fear most people have with windows is that a burglar might break the glass. In most places, however, the sound of breaking glass attracts a lot of attention. And would you want to climb through a window frame with jagged shards of glass? Neither would most burglars.

But occasionally burglars break glass to reach in and unlock a window (or door). If you live where few people would hear (or care about) your windows being broken, or if you just want maximum security, you should be concerned about the type of glass you have.

TYPES OF GLASS

Sheet glass (or "standard window glass") is commonly used in homes because it's inexpensive. It comes in single and double strength; both are light and break easily. When sheet glass breaks, it shatters into jagged shards. You can make your windows stronger and safer by replacing sheet glass with plate glass, tempered glass, laminated glass or tempered plastic.

Plate glass comes in various thicknesses, from about $1/8$-inch to one-inch. It's used in picture windows and sliding glass doors. When it breaks, plate glass shatters into large jagged pieces— which can be dangerous.

Although it can cost twice as much as plate glass, tempered (or "safety") glass is better for exterior doors and windows. It's much harder to break than either sheet or plate glass, and when tempered glass breaks, it shatters into many little (and relatively harmless) pieces.

Laminated glass is two layers of sheet or plate glass bonded to a layer of plastic sandwiched between them. It's hard to break through; some thicknesses can even stop bullets. If laminated glass is broken, the plastic prevents glass pieces from flying around. The big problem with laminated glass is that it can cost ten times as much as plate glass of comparable size.

Tempered plastic is also highly resistant to breaking and shattering. It's clear and can be used to reinforce or replace glass in windows and doors. The main problem with tempered glass is that it discolors and scratches easily.

SKYLIGHTS

A skylight (or "ceiling window") is a vulnerable point of entry because from the ground it's hard to notice someone crawling around the roof of a house.

To secure a skylight you need to make sure the glass is strong and can be locked from inside the house. You may also want to install grills or bars to protect the skylight. Like all windows, a skylight can be protected with burglar alarm sensors (see Chapter 5 for details on using alarms).

WINDOW AIR CONDITIONERS

Some burglars specialize in homes with a window-mounted air conditioner. Most models can easily be removed.

To secure an air conditioner in a window use long mounting

screws. If you have a burglar alarm, use sensors to trigger the system if the air conditioner is moved.

SECURITY FILM

You can also protect glass by having it coated with security film— a transparent liquid that hardens. When applied to the interior surface of a glass window or door, security film fuses with the glass to create a chemically bonded hard-coat finish that makes the glass very hard to break or shatter.

Some types of security film can withstand shots from a sawed-off 12 gauge shotgun blast and blows from hammers and hatchets.

In addition to defending against intruders, security film protects against damage from high winds and earthquakes by preventing glass from flying around a room.

Security film is usually professionally installed. If you use it and plan to have a burglar alarm system installed, be sure to let your alarm installer know. Some types of security films hinder the use of certain alarm sensors.

WINDOW HARDWARE

Three types of hardware help to prevent people from climbing through a window: security shutters, burglar bars and grates (see fig. 5). When shutters are in the closed or locked position, they're

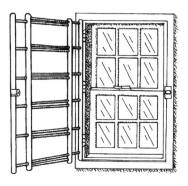

Fig. 5

virtually impenetrable. They're especially useful for small businesses and summer homes.

Burglar bars also offer a lot of security against an attempted break-in, but only use the kind that can be opened quickly from inside your home. Otherwise you could find yourself trapped inside during a fire or other emergency. The best window bars are made of steel and have a steel frame.

Grates are unattractive, but very strong. They're often used on businesses and homes in inner city and other high-crime areas. A grate should be secured with a high-security padlock.

You can buy all types of window hardware from hardware stores and locksmithing shops. Some manufacturers will sell directly to you.

RESOURCES

Security Film

CHB Industries, Inc.

3M Energy Control Products

Weather-Shield Mfg., Inc.

Windows

Andersen Corp.

Atrium Door and Window Co., The

Marvin Windows

Pella Doors and Windows

Window Hardware

Blaine Window Hardware, Inc.

Folding Guard Co.

J. Kaufman Iron Works, Inc.

Vigilante Burglar Bars, Inc.

5.

BURGLAR ALARMS:
DO YOU REALLY NEED ONE?

More than six hundred inmates in an Ohio prison were asked what single thing they would want to protect their homes from burglars. The most popular choice was a dog; the next, a burglar alarm.

In a Security Industry Association survey conducted in 1991, eighty-five percent of the one thousand police officers interviewed said they believe security systems decrease the chances of a home being burglarized.

Burglars and security professionals know that homes with burglar alarms are less likely to be burglarized than those without alarms. No one really knows why; perhaps alarm owners as a group have better locks, doors or windows than most people do. Or perhaps alarm owners generally take more security precautions or live in better neighborhoods.

It's important to put the value of alarms in proper perspective. Although having one is probably beneficial, an alarm shouldn't be seen as more important than good locks, doors and windows. Nor should it be seen as a substitute for being security conscious everyday.

But if you have good locks, doors and windows and want to spend between $500 and $2,000 more for security, then consider installing a burglar alarm.

TYPES OF BURGLAR ALARMS

There are two basic kinds of burglar alarm systems: wireless and hardwired. Both consist of a control panel, a keypad or keyswitch, a sounding device (such as a bell or siren) and sensors.

The big difference is that with a wireless system you don't use wire to connect the sensors to the control panel. In a wireless system the control panel is basically a radio receiver and the sensors are transmitters.

Although a wireless system is generally easier for the do-it-yourselfer to install, it's more prone to false alarms than a hardwired system. And when a wireless system false alarms, you may have a hard time finding the cause. Lightning, airplanes and electronic garage door openers have all been known to cause false alarms. With a hardwired system a false alarm can usually be traced to a broken or loose wire.

With either type of system, the control panel is the brain; it holds programmed information that tells the system how to function. The control panel is usually the most expensive part of an alarm system.

The sensors are strategically positioned throughout a home to detect an intrusion and to alert the control panel. The system can be armed and disarmed with either a keypad or a keyswitch.

In some small systems the keypad and control panel are one unit. Generally all the parts of an alarm system can be bought separately, and mixed and matched with components from other manufacturers.

SENSORS

Sensors (or "detection devices") are installed on doors, windows and floors to detect sound, air movement or body heat. When a person enters a protected area, the sensors immediately inform the control panel. Depending on how the panel has been set to react, it may wait from fifteen seconds to a minute before ordering the system's sirens and lights to activate.

Sensors can cost from a few cents to hundreds of dollars each. Buying them based on price alone, however, can be penny wise but pound foolish. Each type of sensor works best in certain places and under certain conditions. To keep false alarms to a minimum, you need to use the right sensors.

There are two basic types. A *perimeter* sensor is installed on a door, window or other opening to detect an intruder before he enters a room. An *interior* (or "space") sensor protects such open areas as rooms and hallways. It's used to detect an intruder who gets past perimeter sensors.

The most popular perimeter sensor is the magnetic switch (see fig. 6). As its name implies, it consists of a magnet and a switch housed in matching plastic cases. You can buy standard magnetic switches for between one and three dollars per set.

In a typical installation the magnet is mounted on the edge of a door or window, and the switch is aligned about one-half inch away on the frame. If someone pushes the door or window open, the magnet moves out of alignment, activating the alarm.

Three popular types of interior sensors are microwaves, passive infrareds and dual technology.

A microwave detector emits high-frequency radio waves. When

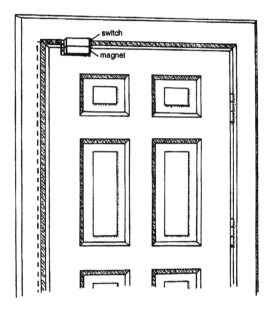

Fig. 6

an intruder enters a protected area, the device senses a change in radio-wave pattern that triggers an alarm. Because radio waves can penetrate walls (and other solid objects), the detector can easily be hidden in a room.

However, the microwave's detection sensitivity is hard to adjust accurately, making it highly susceptible to false alarms. It has been known to mistake many things for intruders, including passing cars, fluorescent lights and radio transmissions.

The passive infrared (or "PIR") sensor is more discerning. It reacts to the infrared radiation (energy in the form of heat) that all living things emit. A typical PIR can monitor an area approximately twenty feet by thirty feet, or a narrow hallway approximately fifty feet long. It doesn't penetrate walls or other objects, so the PIR is easier to adjust than the microwave.

Fig. 7

The biggest drawback to PIRs is that they don't "see" an entire room. They have detection patterns made up of invisible "fingers of protection." (Imagine invisible bicycle wheel spokes.) The spaces outside and between the fingers aren't detected by the PIR. A PIR's detection pattern is determined by its lens (see fig. 7).

Some models have interchangeable lenses that offer a wide range of detection pattern choices. One pattern, called "pet alley," is designed to be used several feet above a floor to allow pets to move about freely without triggering an alarm. Other patterns have invisible fingers of varying lengths that point in numerous directions. Which detection pattern is best depends on which parts of an area you need to protect.

One of the latest types of sensors is dual technology (or "dual-tech"). It combines two sensing technologies into one housing and triggers an alarm only when both simultaneously sense an intrusion. This reduces false alarms.

The most popular dual-tech combines a PIR with a microwave detector. Passing cars and other outside movement that might affect the microwave won't affect the PIR. Conversely, a heater or sunlight on a window might affect the PIR, but won't trigger the microwave. An intruder who walks into a protected area, however, will trigger both technologies.

The problem with dual-techs is price. Some models cost several hundred dollars (two or three times more than PIRs or microwaves alone).

It's seldom necessary to use only the most expensive sensors. Professional installers strategically combine several types. If you do that too, you'll save money and your neighbors will be able to sleep.

MONITORING AN ALARM

An alarm can be monitored locally or remotely. Local monitoring means you or a neighbor listen for the alarm. Remote monitoring means someone at another location is notified when the alarm is activated.

To decide which is best for you, determine if you or a trusted neighbor will always be close by to respond whenever the alarm is activated. If so, you don't need remote monitoring.

The least costly way to have remote monitoring is to connect a tape dialer to your system. When your alarm is activated, the dialer uses your telephone line to call one or more preprogrammed numbers and delivers your recorded message. The idea is that someone—a relative or friend—will get the message and call the police for you. (In some cities the police will respond directly to your recorded message.)

The big problem with a tape dialer is that there's no way to know whether the system was activated by a false alarm. Too many false alarms will probably upset your friends and the police. Some police departments throughout North America levy fines for repeat false alarms. Toronto has an ordinance that allows police to suspend dispatches to an alarm call for 365 days after the fourth false alarm in the same time period.

The best way to avoid repeatedly disturbing your friends and police with false alarms is to use the services of a central monitoring station. When your alarm is activated, a digital dialer sends a coded electronic signal over your phone line to the monitoring station, which is manned twenty-four hours a day.

Depending on the signal received, the monitoring station will either immediately call the police or fire department or will call you to verify the emergency. If you receive a call from the monitoring station and no one answers, or if you (or anyone else) answer without giving your unique code word, the operator will politely hang up and call the police.

Such an arrangement enables you to inform the station if you have a false alarm, but prevents an intruder from stopping the monitoring company from calling for help. The main problem with central station monitoring is cost—between ten and twenty-five dollars per month for the service.

You may also need to pay a fee to your local police department before they'll respond to your alarm. In March 1992 a thirty-eight-year-old woman in Riverside, California, who hadn't paid her alarm permit fee was raped and beaten by an intruder after the police refused to respond to her monitoring company's repeated calls. The police responded only after a neighbor reported hearing screams.

DO-IT-YOURSELF ALARM BUYER'S CHECKLIST

Has the manufacturer been making alarms for at least ten years?

Does the system come with a good warranty?

Does the manufacturer provide monitoring service?

Is the system UL listed?

Is the system operated by a low-voltage transformer?

Does the system come with all the sensors you need?

Does the system come with a backup battery?

Are the bells or sirens loud enough (at least 120 decibels)?

Do the bells or sirens give different sounds for burglary and fire?

Do the bells or sirens automatically shut off after ten minutes?

Does the system's delay feature give you enough time to get out of your home after you arm the system?

PROFESSIONAL ALARM BUYER'S CHECKLIST

Is the installation company licensed or bonded?

Is the installation company a member of the Better Business Bureau, your local chamber of commerce or a trade association?

Has the installation company been in business for at least ten years?

Does the system come with a warranty from the manufacturer and the installation company?

Will all your exterior doors and windows be protected by sensors?

Is the system UL listed?

Does the system come with all the sensors you need?

Does the system come with a backup battery?

Are the bells or sirens loud enough (at least 120 decibels)?

Do the bells or sirens give different sounds for burglary and fire?

Do the bells or sirens automatically shut off after ten minutes?

Does the system's delay feature give you enough time to exit the building after it is armed?

RESOURCES

Burglar Alarms, Do-It-Yourself

Dicon Systems, Inc.

Espion, Inc.

Heath Zenith

Home Automation Laboratories

Transcience

X-10 (USA) Inc.

Burglar Alarms, Professional

ADT Security Systems

AT&T

Dictograph Security Systems

Honeywell, Inc.

6.

THE SAFEST SAFES

Keepsakes, important papers and other hard-to-replace items need special protection from theft and fire. Getting a safe could be a low-cost way of providing that protection; it could also be a costly mistake.

Safes usually offer strong resistance to either fire or burglary—but not both. The design that guards against heat (thin metal walls with insulation sandwiched between) makes a safe easy to force open. The design that makes a safe hard to break into (thick steel and copper walls) allows it to heat up quickly.

Photographs, financial records and other paper items that do not interest thieves can be kept at home in a fire safe, while small amounts of jewelry can be stored in a burglary safe. Storing cash, however, can be tricky because it's both paper and valuable. You could keep it in a burglary safe that's inside a larger fire safe, but I don't recommend that.

It's generally not a good idea to store a lot of valuables in a home safe. No model is completely secure. The paper contents of any safe will burn if exposed to fire for a long enough time. Likewise, any model can be forced open if a burglar with the right tools is given enough time to work. (And the more valuables he believes you might have, the longer he'll be willing to work.)

SAFE RATINGS

To find out how much protection a safe provides, read its rating label. Beware of safes that haven't been rated by an independent agency. For a fire safe, look for the Underwriters Laboratories (UL) or Japanese Industrial Standards (J.I.S.) label. (Their ratings are roughly equivalent.)

To earn a UL (or J.I.S.) rating, a fire safe must meet strict construction guidelines and a sample model must pass several rigorous tests that simulate the extreme conditions of a burning building. Only if the safe's contents are in good condition at the end of the test does that model earn a fire rating.

UL fire ratings include 350-1, 350-2, 125-1 and 125-2. A 350-1 rating means the temperature inside the safe won't exceed 350 degrees Fahrenheit during the first hour of a typical house fire. A safe with a 350-2 rating shouldn't exceed 350 degrees Fahrenheit during the first two hours of a house fire. A 350-class safe is good for storing documents, because paper doesn't char until it's exposed to at least 405 degrees Fahrenheit.

Computer disks are much more sensitive than paper. To store computer disks or magnetic tapes you need a 125-class safe (sometimes called a "media safe"). Some fire safes have both a 350-class compartment and a 125-class compartment.

When looking for a burglary safe, forget about UL and J.I.S. ratings. Their standards for burglary safes far exceed the needs (and bank accounts) of most homeowners. For the best value, look for Broad Form and Mercantile Safe Insurance classifications. Those two independent agencies have overlapping standards based on construction guidelines (not on tests). Their "B" and "C" classifications are common for quality home safes.

B-rated safes have steel or iron doors up to one-inch thick, with steel walls up to one-half inch thick. They sell for between three hundred and six hundred dollars. C-rated safes have steel doors at least one-inch thick with steel walls at least one-half inch thick. They can cost from one thousand to about twenty-five hundred dollars.

SAFE INSTALLATIONS

Before choosing a safe, decide where you want to install it. You have three choices: in a wall, on a floor or in a floor.

A wall safe is the easiest to install, but it offers the least protection against theft. A safe must be very light to rest in a drywall cutout. If a burglar can't rip its door off (in most cases he can), he can just yank the safe out of the wall and carry it away. There's no point in trying to hide a wall safe because burglars routinely look behind pictures, mirrors and other wall hangings.

A floor safe is often used by people who don't want to create any holes in a wall or floor. However, a safe weighing less than 750 pounds should be bolted to a floor. Many burglars use hydraulic pushcarts to lift safes from any floor in a home.

Although it doesn't meet construction guidelines for a UL fire safe, an in-the-floor safe can offer a lot of protection against fire and burglary (see fig. 8). Because it's installed below a floor, and because heat rises, the safe provides more resistance to fire than do wall- or floor-model burglary safes.

Fig. 8

An in-the-floor safe can be permanently installed in a wood or concrete floor, exposing only its door which can be hidden by a rug. These safes come in square, rectangular and cylindrical bodies, and have square or round doors. In making your purchase, note that cylindrical body safes don't provide much storage space and round door models are hard to reach into.

Unfortunately, in-the-floor safes are inconvenient; you have to get on your hands and knees to use them, which can be hard on anyone with a bad back.

Every type of safe has strengths and weaknesses. No model is best for everybody. But if you know what kind of protection you need, and where you want to install the safe, you'll be able to choose the safest safe for you.

SPECIAL FEATURES TO LOOK FOR

One feature to consider when buying a safe is what type of lock it uses. The traditional combination lock with a dial (thirty-six to the left, ninety-three to the right . . .) is the most common, but many people prefer the convenience of a key lock.

Some safes use push-button mechanical or electronic locks. Both types are easy to operate and provide quick access to the safe. The electronic models aren't very popular, however, because people don't like having to constantly change batteries.

When choosing a burglary safe make sure it has relockers. Relockers (also called "relocking devices") are special safeguards against forcible entry attempts.

Another feature of a good burglary safe is hardplate—special material that hinders thieves from drilling a safe open. The more hardplate the better (and the more costly). At the very least, every burglary safe should have hardplate between its lock and dial.

GETTING THE BEST BUY

You'll find the lowest priced safes at department stores and hardware stores. Most will be low-rated (or nonrated) fire safes with few security features.

At a typical locksmith shop you'll find only a few safes. They will be more expensive and of better quality than those in department stores. For the widest selection and competitive prices, go to a shop that specializes in selling and servicing safes. You can find them under "Safes & Vaults" in your telephone directory.

Such places often sell used safes at bargain prices. But it's not a good idea to buy a safe that has been through a fire or has been drilled open. Even if they've been repaired, these safes offer less protection than a safe that was never damaged.

When comparing prices among safes, include delivery and installation charges, which usually cost extra.

SAFE ALTERNATIVES

Any home safe is a compromise between security and convenience. If you don't need to store valuable or hard-to-replace things at home, you may not need a safe. The more important the items, the more you should consider storing them away from home.

You may want to rent a safe deposit box at a bank. The smallest boxes sometimes rent for under twenty dollars per year. Of course, you will only have access to the box when the bank is open.

If you need twenty-four hour access to your valuables, you might want to store them in a private vault. Private vaults, like safe deposit boxes, come in a wide variety of sizes and are very secure, but private vaults are more expensive to rent. Expect to pay between fifty and seventy-five dollars per year for the smallest container at a private vault.

You may be able to offset the fee for a safe deposit box or private vault by obtaining a discount on your homeowner's insurance for the items you store off the premises.

RESOURCES

Private Vaults

National Association of Private Security Vaults

Safes

American Security Products Co.

Buddy Security Systems

Gardall Safe Corp.

Schwab Corp.

Sentry Group

7.

LIGHTING YOUR WAY
TO SAFETY

There's a good reason why most people feel uncomfortable walking

alone on a dark street; criminals often take advantage of the shield

of darkness. About fifty percent of burglaries occur at night.

The proper use of lighting not only reduces your risk of being burglarized, but also allows you to quickly find your keys and open a door at night. This makes you less vulnerable to muggers and other types of criminals who lie in wait.

Penny for penny, lights are the best value in security products —if you know how to choose and use them. The movie *Home Alone* showed excellent examples of how lighting can be used to improve security. The character played by little Macaulay Culkin kept the house well lighted outside at night and used timers creatively inside to make the house seem occupied. (The character must have known that very few burglars will break into a home they think is occupied.)

Lighting can be used with burglar alarms, closed-circuit televisions and other security devices. In addition to keeping criminals away at night, good lighting can help prevent accidental slips and falls, help you get outside quickly during a fire at night and make your home more inviting to your guests.

OUTDOOR LIGHTING

All of your exterior doors and windows should be lit at night. You want to be able to see anyone in your yard, and you want your house numbers to be visible from the street. (The police or fire department may need to see the numbers to find your house quickly.)

If you live near a streetlight, you may not need additional outside lighting. As a rule of thumb, if you can walk outside near your exterior doors and windows at night and read your watch you probably have enough light. Too much light is unnecessary and can be annoying to your guests. People don't like to feel like they're on a Broadway stage while ringing your doorbell.

As a convenience for invited guests—and an inconvenience to intruders—you might want to use *automatic light controls*. These devices use a PIR (see Chapter 5 for details on PIRs) to automatically turn on lights whenever someone nears your door (or pulls into your driveway).

Regardless of the type of lighting device—fixture or bulb—you use outside, make sure it's protected against vandalism. No security device is helpful if it can be easily destroyed. Outside security devices should be installed out of easy reach and protected by weather-resistant housing.

INDOOR LIGHTING

Like outdoor lighting, indoor lighting can make your home safer and more secure at night. Stairs, hallways, bathrooms and other areas that are potentially dangerous are less hazardous when visible. You can use automatic light controls indoors to light certain areas whenever someone walks near them.

Another option is to keep several small night lights (four watts or less each) on twenty-four hours a day. They don't use much electricity. You can also use dimmer switches so that you can adjust the brightness of lights as needed.

When you plan to be away at night, use timers to turn lights on and off in two rooms (such as a bedroom and bathroom), to give the appearance of people walking around.

If you just leave one light on all night, a burglar is more likely to think the house may be empty. If you don't have a timer, leave at least two lights on inside. This will make it hard for a suspicious burglar to be sure no one is home.

To keep indoor lighting from being more helpful to burglars than to you, close your blinds and drapes every evening. The darker the night gets, the easier it will be for passersby to see into your well-lighted rooms and judge the value of your possessions.

TYPES OF LIGHT SOURCES

All light sources are not created equal. To decide which type is best for you, compare the initial costs of fixtures and bulbs (or tubes) to the cost of running the light.

The three types of lights commonly used in homes are standard tungsten, tungsten-halogen and fluorescent. The standard tungsten is what most people call a regular light bulb. It comes in clear and frosted models and works with ordinary house current. Because it doesn't need special fixtures, the initial cost is minimal (just the price of a light bulb), but it can become costly over long periods of time.

A tungsten-halogen (or "quartz-halogen") bulb requires a special fixture and is more expensive than standard tungsten bulbs. It is, however, more cost-effective over the long run because it uses less voltage and lasts longer.

Like the tungsten-halogen bulb, fluorescent tubes are expensive to buy, require special fixtures, and are more energy efficient than a standard bulb. Unfortunately, in some locations, they emit harsh and unappealing light.

HOME LIGHTING CHECKLIST

1. Keep the areas outside your exterior doors and windows well lit at night.
2. Make sure your outside lighting leaves no shadows that will provide cover for burglars (multiple light sources prevent shadows better than a single light source).
3. Use weather-resistant protective covers on outside lights.
4. Immediately report any nonworking streetlight.
5. Keep blinds and drapes closed at night.
6. Either leave some lights on all night or use automatic timers near stairs, hallways and bathrooms.
7. Use timers to turn lights on and off in various rooms whenever you're away at night.

RESOURCES

Automatic Light Controls and Timers

Stanley Home Automation

X-10 (USA) Inc.

Lighting Fixtures

Lightoiler, Inc.

Progress Lighting

Rejuvenation Lamp & Fixture Co.

Sea Gull Lighting Products, Inc.

Task Lighting Corp.

8.

HIGH-TECH/LOW-COST SECURITY

Until recently closed circuit televisions and other sophisticated security devices were rarely used in homes, because the devices were too expensive to install and maintain. But advances in computer technology has been changing that. Today the average homeowner can easily afford a wide variety of high-tech security devices.

CLOSED CIRCUIT TELEVISION SYSTEMS

When you need extra eyes to see what's going on, you may want to use a closed circuit television (or "CCTV") system. It can be used indoors and outdoors to watch small children, see who's at the door, watch a pool area, monitor babysitters and so on.

CCTVs can also be tied into a burglar alarm system, so they can begin monitoring select areas when an alarm is triggered. Some models can be wired directly to a PIR sensor (described in Chapter 5), which activates them, without triggering an alarm, whenever someone enters certain areas.

Although a full-blown CCTV system can cost thousands of dollars, you can buy a basic system for under three hundred dollars. A basic system consists of a camera, a video monitor and a coaxial cable to connect the monitor to the camera. Some basic models designed for home use are small and stylish and include an intercom feature.

CCTV CAMERAS

Just as you can use a photographic camera without knowing much about its inner workings, you don't need to know how television cameras work to use them. Your choice of a camera will depend on whether you need it to monitor brightly lit or dimly lit areas, and how much detail you need the monitor to pick up.

Vidicon cameras are the most common and least expensive. They're reliable and relatively compact. Although they work best in well-lit areas, image burn which causes a ghost-like image to appear, can be a problem. In extreme cases, camera tubes must be replaced.

Plumbicon cameras which are highly sensitive to light and burn-in, come in excellent color models, but require more light for high-quality pictures than Newvicon cameras.

As you might expect, color cameras cost much more than black-and-white models. Color, however, is rarely necessary; even most businesses use black-and-white cameras. If you want to see color, however, you need to make sure your monitor is able to display color.

Monitors

Although you could use your television set to monitor a CCTV camera, a video monitor will give you a clearer and more stable picture. If you want to use your television, make sure your camera has an output switch that allows a choice of RF or CCTV output. The RF position can be used to display a picture on your home television.

The two basic kinds of monitors are standard and high-performance. High-performance monitors show better pictures, allow for finer picture adjustments and last longer. (But remember, picture quality depends as much on the camera as on the monitor.)

For home use, you'll probably want at least a nine-inch black-and-white monitor. If you need to view the monitor from more than ten feet away, however, you'll want a larger model.

Auxiliary Equipment

A basic CCTV system isn't very versatile. The camera just stares at one spot. To provide more coverage, you can mount it on a *pan-and-tilt* unit that will continually move the camera to various positions.

If you have more than one camera, you might want a switcher so you can use one monitor to switch between the scenes of several cameras. Switches come in manual and automatic versions.

If you want to use cameras outdoors, provide protective housings to safeguard them from weather and vandals. Some outside housings are designed for special conditions, such as rain, snow and high humidity.

Getting the Best Buy

CCTV parts can be bought separately, allowing you to save money. However, not all components are interchangeable. Before getting a low-cost monitor, for example, be sure it is compatible with the camera you plan to use.

If you don't feel comfortable mixing and matching parts, you can look for a prepackaged system that contains everything you need. A prepackaged system usually costs less than all the parts would cost if bought separately. It's also easy to install, because everything comes from a single manufacturer.

If you want a CCTV only to see who's at your door, consider getting a home system with an intercom feature.

ANSWERING THE DOOR WHEN YOU'RE AWAY

The newest home intercom systems not only let you answer the door when you're home, but also when you're away—even out of town.

The remote systems connect to your phone line. When the doorbell rings, you pick up the phone and dial a code to talk to the person at the door. You can have separate codes if you use more than one doorbell.

If you're going to be away from home, you can program the system to call you whenever a doorbell is pushed. Then you can talk to a person at your door just as if you were home.

Remote home intercoms are easy to install; they cost between three and four hundred dollars.

CATCHING CROOKS BY PHONE

In the summer of 1991 a burglary ring in Virginia was caught by phone. After making a routine call to a home to make sure it was empty, the thieves broke in and took nearly every valuable in sight

—except a small white box attached to the phone. That box had recorded the thieves' home phone number.

Those thieves are among many who have been tracked down by Caller ID—a new phone service. It allows you to automatically record the date, time and phone number of each call you receive. To use the service you have to pay the phone company a fee (about six dollars a month) and attach your phone to a display device (between twenty-five and one hundred dollars). You can also use a personal computer as your display device.

Caller ID isn't available in all states because some people consider it an invasion of privacy or a violation of wiretap statutes. Most states that allow the service require that all callers have the option of blocking their phone numbers from being displayed. (A caller does so by dialing a code before making a call.)

In states that don't allow Caller ID, you can subscribe to Call Tracing Service, which doesn't require a display device. For about the same monthly fee as Caller ID, you can have the option of having the phone company keep a record of the time, date and caller number for any call you receive.

After hanging up on, for example, an obscene caller, you press a few numbers and a recording will then confirm that the last call you received has been traced. Although the phone company won't release the information to you, the information can be used by the police to catch the caller. One advantage of Call Tracing Service is that callers don't have the option of blocking their phone numbers.

RESOURCES

Aiphone Corp.

Burle Industries, Inc./Security Products Div.

Elmo Manufacturing Corp.

Home Automation Laboratories

Panasonic Communications & Systems Co./Closed Circuit Video
Equipment Div.

Toshiba Video Systems

9.

LEARN NOT
TO BURN

Throughout the nation fire kills about 5,000 people and injures about 100,000 every year—most of them in their own homes—according to the U.S. Fire Administration.

Many people don't worry about being injured in a fire; they

think if one starts they'll just run out. But that's not always possible. Fire quickly depletes air of oxygen and produces poisonous gases that can severely reduce muscle coordination and hamper rational thinking.

Even if you can quickly exit your home during a fire, what about your family, your possessions and your home itself? By taking proper precautions you'll not only decrease the risk of fire, but you'll be better able to handle the situation if one occurs.

CAUSES OF HOME FIRES

The leading cause of home fires is improper use and maintenance of heating equipment (such as portable heaters, space heaters and wood stoves). Just by regularly making sure your heating equipment is in good working order, and always following the manufacturer's operating instructions, you'll greatly reduce the risk of fire.

The second leading cause of home fires—and the leading cause of fire injuries at home—is dangerous cooking practices. Cooking fires are easy to prevent. You should wear short or tight-fitting sleeves, don't lean over the stove, keep the stove top clear and clean, turn handles on pots and pans inward so they won't get knocked off the stove and don't leave the house while cooking.

The biggest cause of home-fire deaths is the careless use of smoking materials. That's because people often smoke when they're not fully alert, such as while drinking alcohol, while watching TV, in bed after sex. . . .

Of course, one way to prevent smoking-related fires is to prohibit smoking in your home. Other measures include paying attention to where ashes fall when smoking, using sturdy and deep ashtrays, dousing butts with water before dumping them in the trash and not smoking in bed or when you're drowsy.

SMOKE AND HEAT DETECTORS

If you were sound asleep and a fire broke out in your home, would the smoke awaken you? Not likely. Most fatal home fires occur between midnight and 4:00 a.m., when people are usually asleep. That's why early warning devices are so important.

Businesses often use heat detectors in areas where heavy smoke is commonplace. But smoke detectors are best for most homes, because smoke can usually be detected before heat. A fire may smolder for hours before bursting into flame.

If you have a burglar alarm you may be able to connect smoke and heat detectors to it. If your system allows that option, use different sounds to indicate fire and burglary. That way, when your alarm sounds, you will know the nature of the emergency.

FIRE EXTINGUISHERS

A fire extinguisher can be helpful for putting out small fires if you use the right type. The wrong type can make the fire worse.

Extinguishers come in four classes, based on the types of fires they're designed to fight. Class A extinguishers are for putting out fires on paper, wood and some plastics. Class AB extinguishers can not only put out those fires, but also fires on grease or oil. Class BC extinguishers aren't for paper, wood or plastics, but can combat fires on grease, oil and electrical equipment.

Because you never know what kind of fire you might face, the best extinguisher for home use is the Class ABC. It can be used to combat all three basic classes of fire as well as combination fires.

In addition to its class, you also need to consider a fire extinguisher's weight. The heavier it is, the more extinguishing materials it will contain. But you don't want one that's too big for you (and others in your home) to handle.

Make sure the fire extinguisher has a pressure dial that enables you to easily determine if the extinguisher is full. You don't want to find out during a fire that it's been leaking and won't work anymore.

Using a Fire Extinguisher

Only fight a fire if it's small and you have an exit door behind you so you can easily get out of the house if necessary.

When fighting a grease fire, stand at least ten feet away from the flames so your extinguisher's stream will be less likely to spread the fire. With other fires, stand as close as you safely can.

With most extinguishers you simply pull out the safety pin, aim the nozzle at the base of the fire (not at the flames) and squeeze the trigger. (But carefully read the instructions that come with your fire extinguisher, because not all models work the same way.)

After your fire extinguisher has been used (even if for only a few moments), immediately take it to a dealer to be recharged.

FIRE SPRINKLER SYSTEMS

Residential fire sprinkler systems are quickly gaining in popularity. They save lives and property by extinguishing a fire before it spreads to other areas of a home.

Contrary to what some people believe, not all sprinklers in a system go off during a fire. Each sprinkler head is designed to react individually. Normally, only those directly over the fire will activate, keeping water damage to a minimum (far less than the damage caused by fire department hoses).

Sprinkler systems are very reliable and rarely go off accidentally. Loss records of Factory Mutual Research show that the probability of a sprinkler discharging accidentally due to a manufacturing defect is only 1 in 16 million sprinklers per year in service.

For as little as $2,000 you may be able to have a fire sprinkler system built into a home under construction. It can cost $4,000 or more to retrofit a system into an existing home. The cost, however, may be offset by insurance discounts. Most states allow discounts of up to fifteen percent of the entire homeowner policy premium for single family residences protected with sprinklers and smoke detectors.

ESTABLISHING AN ESCAPE PLAN

When your smoke alarm goes off, you may not have a lot of time to react. Smoke and fire move quickly. That's why you need an escape plan that everyone in your home is familiar with.

Begin by drawing a floor plan that includes every room in your home. Show the quickest escape routes from each room, along with alternate escape routes. If possible, avoid routes that pass stairwells and open hallways because fire and smoke can collect quickly in such places. For a bedroom above the first floor, install a rope ladder in the window to provide an extra means of escape.

Designate a spot outside your home—such as a place near a streetlight—for everyone to meet. That will allow everyone to know who has escaped and prevent people from needlessly running back into the home.

WHAT TO DO DURING A FIRE

Whenever a smoke alarm goes off, assume you may have a fire. Stay calm and think before you act. You won't have time to undo a lot of mistakes. Your actions will depend on where you are, whether or not you can see fire or smoke and how large the fire is.

If you're in an open space, make sure there's an exit door behind you in case the fire gets out of hand. If you can't position yourself in that way, don't try to put out the fire. You should always have a way out, because a small fire can instantly become large and dangerous.

Only if the fire is small, and you're between the fire and an exit, should you consider trying to extinguish it yourself.

If you put out a fire on a mattress, couch or stuffed chair, call the fire department immediately. Have someone come over to make sure the fire is completely out. Otherwise, you might find your home in flames a few hours later.

If you're cooking and the grease in a pan catches fire, your best option may be to get out of the house and call the fire department. If the fire is small you may be able to put it out by covering the pan with a tight-fitting iron lid and turning the stove off. You might want to use an ABC-class fire extinguisher. But don't pick up a flaming pan to take it to the sink and don't pour water on the pan.

If you're in a room when you hear a smoke alarm, touch the top of the door before opening it. If the door is cold, brace your shoulder against it and slowly open it a few inches. Be prepared for a burst of smoke and flames. If there is no fire between you and an exit, drop to your knees and quickly crawl to that exit. Try to close doors that you pass to slow the spread of the fire.

If you're in a room and the door is hot, don't open it. Stuff rags under the door and in all cracks around it. If possible, splash water on the door (but don't open the door to get water).

If the room gets smoky, take short breaths and breathe only through your nose. Stay low and cover your face with a rag. If possible, crawl to a window and open it at the top and bottom a few inches. This will allow heat and smoke to go out the top of the window, while you breathe fresh air coming in at the bottom. After the smoke clears, close the windows again (unless, of course, you can climb out safely).

If you have a phone in the room call the fire department. Tell the dispatcher your location, the problem and your name—in that order. Don't hang up the phone until you're told to do so; the dispatcher may not have heard you clearly or may need to ask questions.

Once you're out of a burning building, don't go back in before the fire department says you can—not even to save others or pets. Going back in isn't heroic—it's foolish. If you open doors you'll be helping the fire and toxic poisons spread faster.

The best thing you can do after getting out is to make sure the fire department has been called. Although it may seem like an eternity, they'll arrive very quickly. Firefighters have the experience and tools needed to rescue others left in the home.

If everyone knows what to do, you won't need to worry. Anyone who couldn't get out, will be safely behind a closed door waiting for the firefighters to arrive.

FIRE HAZARDS CHECKLIST

Clear out rubbish and old newspapers from your basement, attic, closets and other storage areas.

Make sure no rubbish or furniture is stored near your furnace.

Make sure no curtain or wall hanging in your kitchen can be blown into contact with your stove.

Make sure no aerosol cans or flammable liquids are near heat sources.

Make sure all extension cords are large enough for the appliances they're used for.

Keep electrical cords away from heaters and high-heat sources.

Make sure any electrical cords near water sources are waterproof.

Make sure no electrical cords are frayed.

Make sure your light bulbs don't require more wattage than their fixtures are rated for.

Make sure your chimney is cleaned at least once a year.

With a chimney, use a fire screen that covers the entire front of the fireplace.

Make sure wood or coal-burning stoves are cleaned regularly.

Make sure there is plenty of air space around televisions, stereos and computers.

Make sure all ashtrays you use are deep and have wide edges, so that burning cigarettes can't fall out.

RESOURCES

National Fire Protection Association

National Fire Sprinkler Association, Inc.

United States Fire Administration

10.

DOING BUSINESS
AT HOME SAFELY

The more secure the rest of your home is, the more secure your
home office will be. But a home office has unique security concerns that don't apply to the rest of the house. I have a special

interest in those concerns because I've worked at home for years as a security consultant and freelance writer.

Burglars who know you work at home know someone is there throughout the day and night. That's to your advantage. However, they also know you have computers, printers, fax machines and other easy-to-sell valuables. That combination of factors makes your home less susceptible to amateur burglars, but more susceptible to professional ones.

What you can do to reduce the risk of your home being targeted by burglars depends on the type of business you're in, the layout of your home and how much you want to spend on security.

The best way to eliminate the extra security threat that comes with having a home office is to not let anyone know you work at home. If most of your work is done by mail, you may want to use a post office box.

You may also want to have only your name, and not your address, listed in your local phone directory. Customers or clients will still be able to learn your phone number from the operator, but they won't be able to use the phone book to find out where you live.

If you have an answering machine, don't leave a message that leads people to think you're not home. You might want to say something like, "Hello, I can't answer the phone now. But if you leave your name, number and a brief message, I'll get back to you shortly."

And don't be too trusting of delivery people; some of them sell information to professional burglars. It's best to deal with delivery people at your front door, rather than letting them into your home.

If customers or clients must come to your office, you'll need to keep the rest of your home as separate from the business as possible. A separate entrance can help, but if people must walk through other rooms to get to your office, lock doors and block off areas along the route.

If you need to keep an entrance door unlocked, install a door announcer that will ring whenever someone enters. You may also want to install a convex or dome security mirror near the entrance so you can immediately see anyone who comes in.

Whether people regularly come to your office or not, there are several things you can do to greatly reduce the risk of theft.

1. Have your office in a room where people outside can't see the contents. If necessary, keep your shades or blinds drawn. (There's no need to tempt thieves.)

2. Keep your office windows locked.

3. Keep your office door locked when friends and relatives visit. (Every thief is someone's friend or relative.)

4. Make sure the door to your office is as strong as your home's main exterior door. Both should be solid and equipped with deadbolts. Each door should operate only with its own key.

5. If your phone is equipped with a speed-dialing feature, program it so you can quickly call the police and fire department.

6. When you buy new office equipment don't place the empty boxes out to be picked up by garbage collectors. Break the boxes down and put them in garbage bags.

7. Store important papers in a UL-listed 350-class fire safe.

8. Store important computer diskettes in a UL-listed 125-class media safe; a standard fire safe can't protect diskettes from heat. (See Chapter 6 for details on using safes.)

RESOURCES

Office Supply Catalogs

DAK Industries Inc.

Global Computer Supplies

Secure-It, Inc.

11.

GETTING INSURANCE JUST IN CASE...

Although you can do many things to reduce your risk of burglary and fire, there's no way to eliminate the risks completely. That's why it's important to have insurance that covers losses you can't afford.

Most people with insurance are paying far too much for far too little coverage. They become aware of that only after a burglary or fire. Then, the once friendly insurance agent often becomes cold, legalistic and quick to point out the many shortcomings of a policy.

To get the best homeowner's (or renter's) coverage at the lowest price possible, you need to choose the right agent, understand what you really need and know how to read an insurance policy.

CHOOSING AN AGENT

A good agent can be very helpful if you know your insurance needs. He has a lot of current information at his fingertips that can help you save money. (But he probably won't tell you about everything that's in your best interest unless you ask.)

Although the agent may be friendly, he isn't your friend—any more than the person who sold you your last car is a friend. You and the agent have competing interests—he wants to make money and you want to save money.

Choosing an insurance agent is a lot like choosing any other professional service provider. You want the most knowledgeable and reputable person you can find. Ask your neighbors, friends and business associates about their experiences.

Although most agents have passed a state test, look for one who also has a C.P.C.U. (Chartered Property/Casualty Underwriter) designation. And find out how long the agent has been selling property insurance; the longer the better.

In many cases an agent who works for one company can give you the policy you need. But your odds of getting a good deal are better with an independent agent, who can offer options from various companies.

HOW MUCH COVERAGE DO YOU NEED?

To know how much coverage you need, you have to understand why you need insurance. Insurance is to help you pay for losses that would be too expensive for you to cover. It isn't for making money. It isn't even for replacing everything you own dollar-for-dollar.

Don't be fooled by an agent who tries to sell you a policy that "covers everything." There's no such policy. If your home burned to the ground, no insurance policy would fully cover everything you lost.

You'd be wasting your time if you itemized the cost of every destroyed sock, shoe, book, magazine, cassette tape, compact disc, etc. But a good policy would pay for another house, replace the major items you lost, help you with living expenses while you're getting a new home, and pay for any liability you incurred if someone was injured during the fire.

The Value of Your House

For insurance purposes, the value of your house isn't necessarily what you paid for it. In most cases the value is whatever it would cost to rebuild the house. The figure is adjusted as the cost of building materials and labor changes.

Because a house is rarely totally destroyed, there's usually little reason to insure it for one hundred percent of its value. But many insurance policies require you to keep your home insured for at least eighty percent of its value. If you have less coverage when a disaster hits, the insurance company may have to pay little—or nothing at all.

The Value of Contents

In addition to determining the value of your house, you need to know how much its contents are worth. The Property Inventory Form in Chapter 14 will help you do that.

A homeowner's policy usually includes a standard maximum coverage for contents, based on the amount you're insuring the house for. Unfortunately, that standard coverage may be too little for some items you own and too much for others.

If you own expensive jewelry or a coin collection, for instance, the standard coverage for those items may not be enough. You may need to purchase floater policies for the extra coverage you need.

UNDERSTANDING YOUR POLICY

The best time to learn your coverage, rights and responsibilities under your policy is when you buy it—not when you need to make a claim. When you choose a policy, read it carefully and talk with your agent about parts you don't understand.

Although the language of homeowner's policies can vary greatly from state to state (and from year to year), the following general principles apply in most cases.

The term *named perils* means the policy covers only those perils it specifically lists. Suppose the policy lists wind damage but not water damage, for example, and your home was struck by a hurricane. The insurance company would cover the damage that was caused by the hurricane's wind—but not that caused by water.

An *all-risk* policy is a misnomer. It doesn't cover every risk, but it covers every risk it doesn't specifically exclude. If the policy doesn't list hurricanes, for example, as an exclusion, then it will cover that disaster.

Cash value (or "market value") refers to how much something is worth after taking into account depreciation and wear and tear. A ten-year-old television set, for instance, may have no cash value as far as an insurance company is concerned.

Replacement value is the amount you would have to pay to replace an item with one of equal quality.

WAYS TO GET MORE INSURANCE FOR LESS MONEY

1. The cost of an insurance policy can differ by as much as fifty percent among companies in the same city. It pays to shop around for the best price. (Be sure to get prices from companies that give all the discounts in this list that you qualify for.)

2. Look for a comprehensive all-risk policy rather than a named peril policy, because regardless of how a loss occurs you'll still need coverage.

3. Make sure your policy is for replacement value rather than cash value. Many items depreciate quickly and may have little or no cash value when you need to collect on your insurance.

4. Get the highest deductible you can afford. The more financial responsibility you assume for losses, the lower your premiums will be. You don't want to make a lot of small insurance claims anyway because the insurance company may then refuse to renew your policy.

5. Don't include the value of land when getting your home appraised for a homeowner's policy. Your land isn't likely to be stolen or destroyed by fire.

6. Don't buy double coverage. If an item is adequately insured, there's no advantage in getting another policy for it. Some policies specifically prohibit double coverage. At best, you'll only be able to get each insurer to pay a portion of the loss. Regard-

less of how many policies you have, you won't be paid more than the amount of the loss.

7. Don't insure items for more than they're worth. Although the insurance company may allow you to pay the inflated premiums, the company nearly always has the right to replace an item rather than paying you the listed coverage.

8. It's usually a good idea to increase the standard liability coverage from twenty-five thousand dollars to at least one million dollars. The increased coverage won't cost much, but if you're ever sued by someone who gets hurt on your property you'll be glad you have it.

9. If you have a business in your home, your business property may not be covered under your homeowners policy without a rider. If your business is basically a part-time hobby you may be able to find an insurance company that won't require a rider.

10. Some insurance companies give premium discounts if you have deadbolt locks, smoke detectors, a burglar alarm, a sprinkler system or a safe.

11. Some insurance companies give premium discounts if you keep certain valuables in an insured safe deposit box or private vault.

12. Some insurance companies give premium discounts to senior citizens and nonsmokers.

13. Often you can save money by paying your premiums annually instead of quarterly or semiannually.

14. If you live in an area that has special disasters—such as earth-

quakes or floods—your homeowner's policy may not offer enough protection. You may need additional coverage from the federal government. (Ask your agent about it.)

FEDERAL CRIME INSURANCE

Since 1971 the U.S. government has offered federally subsidized home insurance to residents in eligible states. It protects against financial losses up to $10,000 from burglary and robbery.

The Federal Crime Insurance Program was created because increasing crime rates made it hard for many homeowners and tenants to find and afford crime insurance.

You can obtain low-cost crime insurance from the Federal Insurance Administration if you live in Alabama, California, Connecticut, Delaware, Florida, Georgia, Illinois, Kansas, Maryland, New Jersey, New York, Pennsylvania, Rhode Island, Tennessee, the District of Columbia, Puerto Rico or the Virgin Islands.

Coverage is sold in increments of $1,000. A five percent premium discount credit is given if you have a burglar alarm. At present, you can get a $10,000 policy for $126 annually if you don't have an alarm. The annual premium is $120 if you have an alarm.

RESOURCES

Federal Crime Insurance Program

12.

APARTMENT HUNTER'S
SECURITY CHECKLIST

Apartments have all the security problems of a house, plus a few more. But as a tenant you probably can't (or won't want to) make a lot of permanent changes to the building.

You'll save money and avoid headaches if you carefully evaluate an apartment for security *before* you move in. You'll also have more leverage to get the landlord to make necessary changes. This checklist will help you notice potential problems and better compare the quality of security among different apartments.

___ Is the apartment in a low-crime area?

___ Are most buildings in the neighborhood occupied?

___ Is the neighborhood clean?

___ Are nearby streets well lighted at night?

___ Does the neighborhood have an active crime-watch program?

___ Does the main entrance have a guard, CCTV, intercom or other special security precaution?

___ Are smoke detectors in stairways, corridors, laundry rooms and other common areas?

___ Does the building have a sprinkler system?

___ Is the building clean and well maintained?

___ Are stairways, corridors, laundry rooms and other common areas well lighted?

___ Do all exterior apartment doors open and close easily and fit securely in their frames?

___ Do all exterior apartment doors have single cylinder deadbolts?

___ Are all exterior apartment doors steel or solid-core wood?

___ Are peepholes on all exterior apartment doors?

___ Do all movable apartment windows have keyless locks?

— Are all first- and second-floor windows protected with keyless window barriers?

— Does the apartment have a burglar alarm system?

— Does the apartment have enough smoke detectors?

— Is your mailbox large enough to stay tightly closed with the amount of mail you normally receive?

Extra Considerations for High-Rise Apartments

— Is the fire escape inaccessible from the roof, ground or another building?

— Do elevators have monitored intercoms?

— Are elevators well lighted?

— Do elevators have security mirrors so you can see who's in them before you enter?

13.

BEFORE GOING
ON VACATION

When you're on vacation your home is more vulnerable than ever.
Perhaps that's why more burglaries occur in July and August than
in other months.

To reduce the risk of burglary while you're away, your home should be occupied—or, at least, appear to be occupied.

If you can't find a trusted friend to stay at your home, consider a house-sitting service. You should at least have someone go to your home daily to pick up mail, newspapers and other deliveries. Then you won't need to tell various delivery persons that you'll be away. (The fewer people who know your home is empty the better.)

Another advantage of having someone at your home daily is that if there's snow or mud on the ground the person will leave tracks that burglars notice. The absence of such tracks may inform burglars that no one is home.

Burglary isn't the only thing you need to be concerned about. You probably also don't want your house to burn down. The Vacation Security Checklist in this chapter will help you remember what things you need to do to protect your home from burglary and fire.

VACATION SECURITY CHECKLIST

___ Are your blinds, shades and curtains in their normal night positions?

___ Are all appliances that aren't being used turned off and unplugged?

___ Is the thermostat or air conditioner adequately set?

___ Are your automatic timers set to turn on lights and radios at various times?

___ Is the alarm system armed?

___ Have you told your alarm monitoring company how to reach you—or whom else to contact?

___ Is a trusted friend watching your home?

___ Does the friend have your vacation address and phone number in case of emergency?

___ Is your lawn free of toys, tools, ladders and other property?

___ Will your friend pick up your mail and newspapers everyday?

___ Will someone mow your lawn and shovel your walk?

___ Did you ask your local police department to help keep an eye on your home?

___ Are all valuables in a safe deposit box, with a trusted friend or stored away from home?

___ Are the ringers on your telephone turned off or as low as possible?

___ Is your answering machine properly set?

___ Are paints, cleaning fluids and other flammables properly stored?

___ Is garage door locked from inside with its automatic opener turned off?

___ Are all windows and doors locked?

14.

TOP 20 NO-COST
SECURITY MEASURES

1. Always lock your doors and windows when you leave home—even if you're only going next door or plan to be away for a short time. You could be out longer than you anticipated.

2. Never include your name or home address on your key tags. If

your keys are lost or stolen a burglar may be able to use them before you can rekey your locks.

3. Never give a stranger your house keys. Before you give your car keys to a valet or parking lot attendant, remove your house keys from the ring.

4. Never try to hide a door key outside. Burglars know many people do that, and it won't take them long to find your favorite hiding spot.

5. Consider all strangers at your door to be criminals until they prove otherwise. Never assume they're who they claim to be.

Ask for identification, but don't open your door to get it. Tell them that you need to make a quick phone call to verify the identification. Then make the call. Most burglars won't be at your door when you hang up.

If a stranger claims to work for a utility company, delivery service or police department, look out your window for a marked vehicle.

6. Never assume strangers on the phone are who they claim to be. The phone gives crooks maximum anonymity while trying to get (or verify) information needed to rip you off.

It's safer to not participate in telephone surveys of any kind, but if your need to be helpful overtakes your need to be safe (heaven forbid!), get the stranger's number and call back to answer questions.

7. Engrave as much of your property as possible with your

driver's license number or social security number, and use "Operation I.D." (or similar) window stickers to show would-be burglars that your property is marked.

That not only makes your property less valuable to a thief, but it also helps the police recover the items. You may be able to borrow engraving equipment and obtain window stickers from your police department.

8. Keep bushes and shrubbery trimmed so a burglar can't hide behind them while breaking into your home.

9. Never leave notes on your door that might make a burglar think you're not home. Tell your friends not to leave notes on your door.

10. Discuss your crime prevention measures with people only on a need-to-know basis. The fewer people who know how you protect your home the better.

11. Post the emergency numbers of your police and fire departments in your bedroom near the telephone. If your phone has a speed-dialing feature, program those numbers into it.

12. Make sure your house numbers can be easily seen from the street during the day and night. You don't want the police or fire department to have a hard time finding your home.

13. Join a neighborhood crime-watch program. When neighbors work together to look out for suspicious activity they not only deter burglars, but also help catch them. (To find out if your

neighborhood has a crime-watch program, call your local police department's crime prevention officer.)

14. Design an escape plan to be used during a fire. Make sure everyone in the home knows the plan.

15. Don't smoke on a bed or couch if you're drowsy or have been drinking alcohol.

16. Keep the areas around your furnace, water heater and space heaters clean and free of debris.

17. Store flammable liquids in metal containers away from heat sources.

18. Quickly repair or replace frayed electrical cords.

19. Keep a current inventory of all your property, and store it in a safe deposit box or private vault. The inventory will be helpful if your home is burglarized or catches fire. (You can make copies of the Property Inventory form in this chapter for your personal use.)

20. Conduct a complete security survey when you move into a home, and every six months thereafter. This will keep you aware of changing security needs. (You can make copies of the Home Security Survey form in Chapter 15 for your personal use.)

PROPERTY INVENTORY

Name(s) _____

Address _____

Driver's License No. _____   Social Security No. _____

CREDIT CARD INFO.

Name _____   Issued by _____

Card No. _____   Expiration Date _____

Phone No. _____

Name _____   Issued by _____

Card No. _____   Expiration Date _____

Phone No. _____

Name _____   Issued by _____

Card No. _____   Expiration Date _____

Phone No. _____

Name _____   Issued by _____

Card No. _____   Expiration Date _____

EQUIPMENT

Item	Model Number	Serial Number	Place Purchased	Date Purchased	Cost

15.

CONDUCTING YOUR OWN
HOME SECURITY SURVEY

You can get a free home security survey from just about any lock-smith or alarm installation company, but their focus will be on security needs they can help you with and they'll try to sell you whatever they can—whether you need it or not.

You can also get a free survey from some police departments, but few police officers specialize in residential fire and crime prevention. For a complete and unbiased survey you'll have to pay an independent security consultant thousands of dollars—or you can conduct it yourself.

With this book, you should have no trouble conducting a home security survey. Use the checklist in this chapter to make sure you don't miss anything. Here are some professional tips that might also help.

When conducting a home security survey I look for all the ways someone may be able to break into the home, and I figure out the most cost-effective ways to prevent such break-ins without creating fire hazards.

First, I walk around the outside of the home (including attached buildings). I pay special attention to all doors, windows and other openings. I also look for bushes, trees and other objects that a burglar may be able to hide behind.

I notice what property is left outside, such as ladders or tools. I also consider whether or not the home can easily be located by the police or fire department. Then I climb on the roof to look for skylights, windows or other openings.

Before going inside the house, I have a list of every way a burglar could attempt to break in. I know which ways would be easiest and which would be hardest.

Then I go through each room checking the doors, windows,

vents and other openings. I determine the strengths and weaknesses of each room. I consider how easily my clients can get out during a fire. I look for fire hazards. I also talk to my clients about what security measures have been taken (engraving of valuables, inventory of property, rekeying of locks, etc.).

After my survey is completed, I talk with my clients about ways to improve their security. What do I say to them? If you've read the other chapters in this book, you already know.

HOME SECURITY SURVEY

HOME EXTERIOR	EXCELLENT	GOOD	POOR
Shrubbery/bushes (low)			
House number's visibility			
Mailbox location/size			
Exterior lighting			
Exterior door #1 strength			
Exterior door #1 locks			
Exterior door #1 strike box			
Exterior door #1 peephole			
Exterior door #2 strength			
Exterior door #2 locks			
Exterior door #2 strike box			
Exterior door #2 peephole			
Exterior door #3 strength			
Exterior door #3 locks			
Exterior door #3 strike box			
Exterior door #3 peephole			
Walls			

HOME EXTERIOR	EXCELLENT	GOOD	POOR
Roof			
Garage door			
Garage windows			

HOME INTERIOR

Special door #1 strength			
Special door #1 locks			
Special door #1 strike box			
Special door #2 strength			
Special door #2 locks			
Special door #2 strike box			
Sliding glass door			
Other interior doors			
Window types			
Window locks			
Skylights			
Basement windows			
Smoke detectors			
Fire extinguishers			

GENERAL CONSIDERATIONS

Burglar alarm			
Property engraving and inventory list			
Automatic timers			
Safe			
Safe deposit box or private vault			
Homeowner's Insurance			

NOTES:

16.

RESOURCE DIRECTORY

If you find that any of the addresses or phone numbers listed have been changed, please let me know. I'll send you my latest resource directory if you enclose a stamped self-addressed envelope (U.S. postage). My mailing address is: Bill Phillips, P. O. Box 2044, Erie, PA 16512-2044.

SOURCES OF SECURITY PRODUCTS

ABLOY SECURITY INC.
6015 Commerce, Ste. 450
Irving, TX 75063
214/753-1127
800/367-4598

ADT SECURITY SYSTEMS
300 Interpace Pkwy.
Parsippany, NJ 07054
201/316-1000

AIPHONE CORP.
1700 130th, NE
Bellevue, WA 98004
206/455-0510
800/426-1081

AMERICAN SECURITY
PRODUCTS CO.
11925 Pacific Ave.
Fontana, CA 92335
714/685-9680

ANDERSEN CORP.
Bayport, MN 55003
612/439-5150

ASSA HIGH SECURITY
LOCKS
103-00 Foster Ave.
Brooklyn, NY 11236
718/927-2772

AT&T
5 Wood Hollow Rd.
Parsippany, NJ 07054
800/222-3111

ATRIUM DOOR AND
WINDOW CO., THE
P.O. Box 226957
Dallas, TX 75222
214/634-9663

BLAINE WINDOW
HARDWARE, INC.
12319 Blaine Dr., RD 4
Hagerstown, MD 21740
301/797-6500
800/678-1919

ROOKFIELD INDUSTRIES,
INC.
99 West Hillside Ave.
P.O. Box 548
Thomaston, CT 06787
203/283-6211

BUDDY SECURITY
SYSTEMS
1350 S. Leavitt St.
Chicago, IL 60608
312/733-6400
800/886-8688

BURLE INDUSTRIES, INC.
Security Products Div.
1000 New Holland Ave.
Lancaster, PA 17601
717/295-6123

CHB INDUSTRIES, INC.
92 Lakewood Ave.
Ronkonkoma, NY 11779
516/981-2746
800/220-2525

DAK INDUSTRIES, INC.
8200 Remmet Ave.
Canoga Park, CA 91304
818/888-8220
800/325-0800

DICON SYSTEMS, INC.
719 Clayson Rd.
Toronto, ON
Canada M9M 2H4
416/745-6938

DICTOGRAPH SECURITY
SYSTEMS
21 Northfield Ave.
Box 3017
Edison, NJ 08818
201/225-4433

FEDERAL CRIME
INSURANCE PROGRAM
P.O. Box 6301
Rockville, MD 20849
301/251-1660
800/638-8780

DON-JO MFG.
P.O. Box 929
Sterling, MA 01564
800/628-8389

FOLDING GUARD CO.
2101 S. Carpenter
Chicago, IL 60608
312/829-0700

ELMO MANUFACTURING
CORP.
70 New Hyde Park Rd.
New Hyde Park, NY 11040
516/775-3200
800/654-7628

GARDALL SAFE CORP.
219 Lamson St.
P.O. Box 30, Eastwood Sta.
Syracuse, NY 13206
315/432-9115
800/722-7233

ESPION, INC.
137 California St.
Newton, MA 02158
800/548-7313

GLOBAL COMPUTER
SUPPLIES
11 Harbor Park Dr., Dept. 32
Port Washington, NY 11050
800/845-6225

HEATH ZENITH
455 Riverview Dr.
Benton Harbor, MI 49022
616/429-5499

LIGHTOILER, INC.
100 Lighting Way
Secaucus, NJ 07094
201/864-3000

HOME AUTOMATION
LABORATORIES
5500 Highlands Pkwy., Suite
450
Smyrna/Atlanta, GA 30082
404/319-6000
800/466-3522

M.A.G. ENG. & MFG. CO., INC.
15261 Transistor Lane
Huntington Beach, CA 92649
714/891-5100
800/624-9942

HONEYWELL, INC.
Honeywell Plaza
Minneapolis, MN 55408
612/870-5200

MARVIN WINDOWS
P.O. Box 100
Warroad, MN 56763
800/346-5128

J. KAUFMAN IRON WORKS,
INC.
1685 Boone Ave.
Bronx, NY 10460
212/991-5400
800/442-GATE

MEDECO SECURITY LOCKS,
INC.
P.O. Box 3075
Salem, VA 24153
703/380-5000

MEISTER ATLANTA CORP.
3673 Clairmont Rd.
Atlanta, GA 30341
404/451-9700

MUL-T-LOCK CORP.
54-45 44th St.
Maspeth, NY 11378
718/706-0666
800/622-LOCK

NATIONAL ASSOCIATION
OF PRIVATE SECURITY
VAULTS
135 W. Morehead St.
Charlotte, NC 28202

NATIONAL FIRE
PROTECTION ASSOCIATION
1 Batterymarch Park
P.O. Box 9101
Quincy, MA 02269
617/770-3000

NATIONAL FIRE
SPRINKLER ASSOCIATION,
INC.
Robin Hill Corporate Park
P.O. Box 1000
Patterson, NY 12563
914/878-4200

NEW ENGLAND DOOR AND
LOCK CO., THE
46 Chestnut St.
Norwalk, CT 06854
203/866-9283

PANASONIC
COMMUNICATIONS &
SYSTEMS CO.
Closed Circuit Video
Equipment Div.
1 Panasonic Way
Secaucus, NJ 07094
201/392-4429

PEACHTREE DOORS, INC.
4350 Peachtree Industrial Blvd.
Norcross, GA 30071
404/497-2000

PROGRESS LIGHTING
Erie Avenue & G Streets
Philadelphia, PA 19134
215/289-1200

PEASE INDUSTRIES, INC.
7100 Dixie Highway
Fairfield, OH 45014
800/543-1180

REJUVENATION LAMP &
FIXTURE CO.
901 N. Skidmore
Portland, OR 97217
503/249-0774

PELLA DOORS AND
WINDOWS
Rolscreen Co.
102 Main Street
Pella, IA 50219
515/628-1000

ROTON CORP.
Div. Hager Hinge
139 Victor
St. Louis, MO 63104
314/772-4400
800/325-9995

PINECREST
2118 Blaisdell Ave.
Minneapolis, MN 55404
800/443-5357

SCHLAGE LOCK CO.
P.O. Box 3324
San Francisco, CA 94119
415/467-1100

SCHWAB CORP.
3000 Main St.
Lafayette, IN 47902
317/447-9470
800/428-7678

SEA GULL LIGHTING
PRODUCTS, INC.
301 W. Washington St.
P.O. Box 329
Riverside, NJ 08075
609/764-0500

SECURE-IT, INC.
18 Maple Ct.
East Longmeadow, MA 01028
413/525-7039
800/451-7592

SENTRY GROUP
P.O. Box 399001
Miami Beach, FL 33139
716/381-4900
800/828-1438

SIMPSON DOOR CO.
400 Simpson Ave.
P.O. Box 210
McCleary, WA 98557
206/495-3291

STANLEY HARDWARE
Div. of The Stanley Works
195 Lake St.
New Britain, CT 06050
800/262-2161

STANLEY HOME
AUTOMATION
Div. of The Stanley Works
41700 Gardenbrook
Novi, MI 48050
313/344-0070

TASK LIGHTING CORP.
910 E. 25th St.
P.O. Box 1094
Kearny, NE 68848
800/445-6404

3M ENERGY CONTROL
PRODUCTS
3M Center
St. Paul, MN 55144
612/733-5144

TOSHIBA VIDEO SYSTEMS
Div. of Toshiba America
Consumer Products
82 Totowa Rd.
Wayne, NJ 07470
201/628-8000
800/537-7045

TRANSCIENCE
179 Ludlow St.
Stamford, CT 06902
203/327-7810
800/243-3494

UNITED STATES FIRE
ADMINISTRATION
Office of Fire Prevention and
Arson Control
16825 South Seton Ave.
Emmitsburg, MD 21727

VIGILANTE BURGLAR
BARS, INC.
Port Chester, NY 10573
212/328-3700

WEATHER SHIELD MFG., INC.
531 N. 8th St.
Medford, WI 54451
800/365-1365

X-10 (USA) INC.
91 Ruckman Rd.
Box 420
Closter, NJ 07624
201/784-9700
800/526-0027

USING THE YELLOW PAGES

PRODUCT	YELLOW PAGES HEADINGS
Burglar/Fire Alarms	Burglar Alarm Systems; Fire Alarm Systems; Locks & Locksmithing
CCTV Equipment	Security Control Equipment & Supplies
Doors	Building Materials—Retail; Doors; Windows
Fire Extinguishers	Fire Extinguishers; Fire Protection Equipment & Supplies
Lights	Building Materials—Retail; Light Bulbs & Tubes; Lighting Fixtures—Retail
Locks	Building Materials—Retail; Hardware—Retail; Locks & Locksmithing
Safes	Hardware—Retail; Locks & Locksmithing; Safes & Vaults
Smoke Detectors	Building Materials—Retail; Hardware—Retail; Locks & Locksmithing
Sprinkler Systems	Fire Protection Equipment & Supplies; Sprinklers—Automatic—Fire
Window Barriers	Building Materials—Retail; Locks & Locksmithing; Security Control Equipment & Systems
Window Security Film	Security Control Equipment & Systems; Window Tinting & Coating; Windows
Windows	Building Materials—Retail; Doors; Glass—Auto, Plate, Windows, Etc.

U.S. CITIES RANKED BY BURGLARY RISK*

RANK/CITY	1990 BURGLARIES PER 1,000 HOUSEHOLDS	PERCENTAGE CHANGE FROM 1985–1990
1. Atlanta	61	+21
2. Fort Worth	61	−8
3. Dallas	56	−1
4. San Antonio	55	0
5. Miami	55	+11
6. Phoenix	54	−2
7. New Orleans	52	+37
8. Detroit	51	−36
9. Austin	50	+17
10. Buffalo	50	+37
11. Albuquerque	50	−6
12. Fresno	49	−23
13. Charlotte, NC	47	+21
14. Jacksonville	46	+17
15. Kansas City, MO	46	+4
16. Oklahoma City	46	−20
17. St. Louis	46	−18
18. Columbus, OH	45	+27
19. Minneapolis	44	−16
20. Houston	44	−2
21. Memphis	42	−10
22. Honolulu	42	−15
23. Tucson	42	−23

* Sources of information: Uniform Crime Reports 1990, by the U.S. Department of Justice and U.S. Census Bureau.

24. El Paso	40	+6
25. Tulsa	38	−11
26. Long Beach, CA	37	−9
27. Portland, OR	36	−49
28. Cleveland	35	−10
29. Sacramento	35	−44
30. Baltimore	35	+2
31. Boston	34	−10
32. Toledo	33	−6
33. Indianapolis	33	−6
34. Nashville	31	−2
35. Oakland	30	−47
36. Seattle	30	−38
37. Chicago	29	−12
38. Pittsburgh	28	−16
39. Milwaukee	28	+14
40. San Diego	27	−17
41. Denver	27	−53
42. New York City	25	−15
43. Cincinnati	25	+3
44. Washington, DC	25	+9
45. Omaha	25	−9
46. Los Angeles	24	−29
47. Philadelphia	24	+14
48. Virginia Beach	20	+3
49. San Jose	16	−46
50. San Francisco	14	−27

CANADIAN PROVINCES/TERRITORIES
RANKED BY BURGLARY RISK*

RANK PROVINCE/TERRITORY	1990 RESIDENTIAL BREAKING AND ENTERINGS PER 100,000 POPULATION
1. Northwest Territories	1,576
2. Yukon	1,092
3. British Columbia	1,046
4. Quebec	1,042
5. Manitoba	905
6. Saskatchewan	810
7. Alberta	798
8. Ontario	631
9. Nova Scotia	600
10. New Brunswick	539
11. Newfoundland	388
12. Prince Edward Island	313

* Source of Information: Canadian Crime Statistics 1990, by the Canadian Centre for Justice Statistics.

ABOUT THE AUTHOR

Bill Phillips is a security consultant and freelance writer who specializes in residential security. A graduate of the National School of Locksmithing and Alarms (New York City branch), he has worked throughout the United States in many security positions, including alarm-systems technician, safe technician and locksmith.

Mr. Phillips is the author of five books including *Home Mechanix Guide to Home Security* (John Wiley & Sons) and *Professional Locksmithing Techniques* (TAB Books/McGraw-Hill). He has also written technical manuals that are used for training law-enforcement officers and locksmiths.

Mr. Phillips has been a contributing editor of several security-related professional journals, and is the "Home Security" columnist for *Home Mechanix* magazine. His articles also appear in *Consumers Digest, Crime Beat, Locksmith Ledger International, Safe and Vault Technology Special Report,* and other magazines.

Questions and comments about *Hassle-Free Home Security* may be sent to:

Bill Phillips
P.O. Box 2044
Erie, PA 16512-2044
CompuServe mail: 73234, 1465
GEnie mail: B.Phillips3